A World of Homes

Heather Hammonds

Contents

Chapter 1

Our House

My family has a new house. It is made of bricks. It has two floors. There are many new houses on our street.

Uncle Sanjay drew the plans for our new house. Then builders built the house for us.

Uncle Sanjay is going on a vacation. He will visit lots of different houses around the world.

He will send me some e-mails. He will take pictures of the houses so I can see them, too.

Chapter 2

Homes on Stilts

Hi, Anil!

I have arrived in Thailand. I am staying in this house on stilts. The house is beside a river. The stilts keep the house safe and dry when the water in the river gets higher.

Uncle Sanjay

Sometimes it is very hot in Thailand. Air blows underneath stilt houses to help keep them cool.

Chapter 3

Homes of Grass

Hi, Anil!

I have traveled to South Africa. I visited this round house. It has a frame of big sticks and is covered with grass.

The house has a hard, shiny floor. The floor is made of **compost** that has been rubbed with stones.

These grass houses
are built by the **Zulu**
people. Some Zulus live
in grass houses. Most
live in houses made
of brick or wood.

Chapter 4

Underground Homes

Hi, Anil!

I am now in Tunisia. It is very hot here. The homes in this **village** have been dug out of the ground. They are called cave homes.

The ground around the cave homes helps keep them cool inside during hot days.

Each of the homes in this village has its own **courtyard**.

Chapter 5

Homes by the Sea

Hi, Anil!

I am staying on an island in Greece. All the houses here are painted white. The white paint helps **reflect** the heat from the hot sun.

The houses are all shaped like boxes. They are very beautiful.

Many of the houses on this island have blue doors and window frames. Blue is thought to be a lucky color by those who live on the island.

Chapter 6

Thatched Roofs

Hi, Anil!

I have traveled to a village in England. The houses here are made of bricks, but their roofs are made of special kinds of straw. The roofs are called **thatched roofs**.

Thatched roofs are thick and strong. They last for many years.

A person who builds thatched roofs is called a thatcher.

Chapter 7

A Hotel of Snow and Ice

Hi, Anil!

I am staying at this **hotel** in Canada. It is made of snow and ice. Everything inside the hotel is made of ice, too.

The hotel opens in winter. It closes in spring because it melts! A new hotel is built every year.

Brrr!

This igloo is a home made from blocks of snow. Igloos are made by the **Inuit** people of Canada. Today most Inuit live in homes made from bricks or wood.

Chapter 8

City Homes

Hi, Anil!

I am now in New York City. There are lots of tall buildings here. I am staying in this big **apartment** building. Many families live in this building. Each family has their own apartment.

Some apartments in New York are called walk-up apartments. This is because you must walk up some stairs to get to them.

Chapter 9

A Home of Wood and Earth

Hi, Anil!

I am now in the Southwest. I visited this home of wood and earth. It is called a hogan.

Hogans have one big room inside. They also have a door that faces the sunrise. This is so the family inside can greet the rising sun each day.

Hogans are built by the
Navajo people. Some
Navajo live in hogans.
Many live in homes
made of bricks or wood.

Chapter 10

Bricks of Mud and Straw

Hi, Anil!

I have traveled to Mexico. These houses are made of mud bricks. Straw is put into the mud bricks to make them stronger. Then the bricks are dried in the sun.

After the houses are built, the brick walls are covered with more mud. This makes them look smooth.

This kind of mud brick
house can only be built
in dry places. Lots of rain
would wash the bricks away.

Chapter 11

A Rain Forest Home

Hi, Anil!

I am in the rain forest in South America. Many families live together in this big home. It is called a shabono.

The shabono is made of vines, branches, and leaves from the rain forest. It is built in a big circle. Each family has a part of the shabono for their own.

My vacation is almost over. See you soon!

Uncle Sanjay

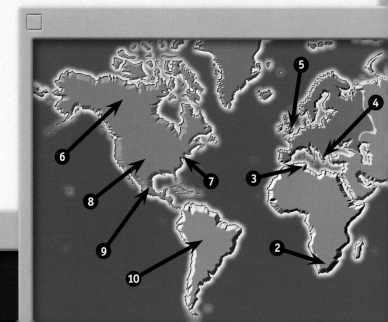

Shabonos are built by the **Yanomami** people. Most Yanomami live in the rain forest of South America.

1	Thailand	**6**	Canada
2	South Africa	**7**	New York City
3	Tunisia	**8**	The Southwest
4	Greece	**9**	Mexico
5	England	**10**	South America

Glossary

apartment a room or group of rooms that people live in within a larger building

compost a mix of decayed materials

courtyard an open space next to a house or other building

hotel a place where travelers can pay to stay

Inuit a group of people who live in Canada

Navajo Native Americans living mainly in New Mexico, Arizona, and Utah

reflect to bounce off something

thatched roofs roofs on houses or other buildings that have been made of straw or reeds

village a very small town

Yanomami native people living in the rain forest of South America

Zulu a group of people who live in South Africa

Index

24